A Wish Like You

Ria Gupta Choudhary

BookLeaf Publishing

India | USA | UK

Made with ❤ on the BookLeaf Publishing Platform
www.bookleafpub.in
www.bookleafpub.com

Dedication

My family, my husband and my close friends have loved my poetries and have always encouraged and motivated me to keep going and pursue my dreams. The inspiration and confidence which I get from their appreciation is the driving factor towards the thoughts which I have penned down in this book. This book is my long cherished dream, hope you all love it.

-Anokhi

Preface

I have tried to pour my heart out in this book with utmost dedication and love. I believe that many people will be able to relate with the emotions and feelings that I have tried to carve out in this book. Being an amateur author, this book is a dream. Hope to receive lots of love on this.

- Anokhi

Acknowledgements

To all my supporters and motivators, thank you for all the love, support and appreciation.

1. A dreamscape

Amidst the hustle and bustle of my life
My soul wanders for peace and solace
It gets intrigued just by the sight of yours
Puzzled how enthralling and boisterous can it get
Without failing to maintain its calmness
You somewhere pacify the roaring clamour inside me
which provokes me to bloom even in misery
You push me away from the clumsy thoughts,
In which I was ever since caught
You set me free from my carved entangled proximity
By showing me the glimpses of reality in your vicinity
You have been the constant healer in a world full of
temporaries
Never failing to mesmerize us with your spell bound
beauty
seeming to be imaginary.

2. Solitude

Her mind was full of confusion
like the fickle waves of the ocean
she constantly struggled with her emotions
trying to get rid of them
without any explosion
her heart had become cold and frozen
maybe because,
yet again she was not chosen.

3. A night of illusion

I resent the nights
for its loneliness and emptiness
driving me towards a plethora of thoughts
all about you
which I constantly run away from
Yet, I adore the nights
for its peace and calmness
giving me those moments to live by,
though in my thoughts
which I have always longed for.

4. Won't it matter to you ?

Those feelings which I have caged all these years
all by myself in my heart
don't let them go away
because they are meant forever to stay
they deserve to be loved back now
have been reserved for all these years,
don't ask me how
your mere thought until now,
gives them jitters
hoping that someday you'll acknowledge them
with your love and not bitter
they still dream about being with you in the lonely
nights
staring at the moon which shines all beamy and bright
but now, it's patience is being tested
after all, how long will they remain congested
so, what if, I tell you that my feelings for you want to get
released from you
still, wont it matter to you?

5. An incessant wait

I never expected I would ever fall for you
Maybe it was just meant to happen,
which I wish I earlier knew
These feelings were something,
which I never had felt before
If only I could make you feel the same,
maybe a little less if not more
As life happened, our ways got parted,
With a deep down hope of again getting united
Call it destiny or a lesson to be learnt,
You re-entered my life and it all got turned
Oh how I wish to be always there for you
Wanting you to seek only me,
be it at midnight or noon
Oh how I wonder that I understand you better,
Maybe you'll realise it soon,
if not today, then later
Oh how I wish to heal all your scars
By embracing you forever in my arms
My eyes just can't bear your eyes drenched

My heart goes racing, which can go for you to any
extent
Oh how I wish that your smile never gets faded away,
You get whatever you desire, that's all I pray.
I somewhere know that you and me might not happen,
Still hoping that something could actually make it
happen
I know, I might never be able to express this to you,
no matter how much and how long I crave.
But, this is just for the thing, I wish, we could ever have,
if not now, then, maybe after yet another wait.

6. The First meet ?

Though it was not their first meet
For her, it was not less than a soulful feel
The reason was that they were meeting after ages
Making her revisit her old story of which she had long
closed pages
The excitement of being with him she could not express
The anxiety of being with him she could not digest
Her admiration for him knew no bounds
She couldn't understand whether she was lost in him or
was found
The time spent together didn't seem too long
Oh how she wished at that moment for it to prolong
The tunes did nothing but made her feelings more
restless
Only to make her realise that her crave for him seemed
endless
Amidst she got lost in her countless thoughts
Since she was actually living the moment which she had
thought was put at a halt
She couldn't help from falling for him a bit again

Ofcourse, knowing, that he wouldn't reciprocate to her
feelings yet again
The meet finally got over
leaving her confused
whether they have drifted apart
or have actually come closer.

7. A tagged fear

For a beautiful mess that you are
but all disguised in tranquility
stop caging yourself
with the fear of odds
or being judged
because that's my dear,
where lies your liberty.

8. Heart's quest

My heart searches for solace in your
arms
That's the only thing which can keep me calm
My heart searches for me in your eyes forever
Always wishing that nothing could do us apart ever
My heart searches for the real you
Always pondering about the things which
you do
My heart searches for the love it wants,
from no one else but YOU.

9. A bitter pleasure

You once told me that, maybe, we could have a thing
someday
That one statement of yours was enough
to make me wait for you,
until infinity,
without any dismay.

10. A symphony of love

Like a deserted island was I,
who longed for a deep proximity
you came in as a permanent inhabitant
and held me tight in your never ending captivity
though tried to set free umpteen times
I kept drifting towards you
making it a love symphony.

11. Crave it - Vacate it

The irony which smacks you the most
keeping you completely entangled and engrossed
when the heart still yearns for you
but the mind wants to get rid of the chaos created by you
Oh how you have left me totally bewildered
as if all my whimpers seem to be unheard.

12. A forbidden desire

You made me fall in love
with my own flaws
still, you couldn't ever fall for me
though, even the stars could witness
the wait in my eyes for you
why is it that
you were always unable to see?

13. An enticing thought

I allowed you in my life again
only with the condition of
not falling for you again,
but I guess,
my loneliness craves for solace
only from you,
making you irresistible for me even now
as much as it was before.

14. Hopes of a parallel world

Let's just elope from everyone,
with the passing time
getting crazy for each other,
with the magic of divine wine
embraced in each other's arms,
tapping to the soulful music,
just like the chimes
so that until infinity,
without any worry,
I could be yours and
you could be mine.

15. Hold me like

Hold me like
I get drowned in your eyes forever
Giving me a moment of lifetime
which I have experienced never
Hold me like
The only thing between us is your soothing breathe
Resisting and stopping me everytime, I think to leave
Hold me like
I get mesmerized by you all over again
My racing heartbeats could feel yours in the drizzling
drops of rain
Hold me like
You and I are the best thing that could ever happen
So that nothing could ever do us apart
and everything else is just forgotten.

16. Be my serenity

While in distress,
I wandered for peace everywhere
the hunt yet again halted at you
comforting and healing me such,
making me believe with all your gush,
as if the pile of dismay and sombre
in my life, were never there.

17. A blissful love

Love, which is defined by no boundaries,
is a deeply rooted yearned emotion
don't get bothered by those rotten minds
who simply try to defame it by their obscure allegations
Instead, feel lucky about the fact
that you have found the true love of your life
because dear, in this cruel world,
having found someone,
epitomises a crown of lovely pride.

18. Everyday blues

Sometimes you are so much in love
that you want to get out of love.

Sometimes what bothers is the feeling
of not feeling that feeling.

Have you ever bothered
the heart which crossed miles for someone,
how can you expect it to come back to you within a
fraction.

Love completes you even with all its flaws, its beauty, its
sustenance, even in the absence of togetherness.

Efforts are good
but doesn't it feel better when someone is initiates them
for you.

19. Because you are worthy

There are millions of stars
against only one moon in the sky,
but that nowhere diminishes the importance of stars,
people are still mesmerized by them
because they make them do so with their elegance and
sparkle

So is love
Lett your love for someone blossom you
and not degrade
If it's meant to happen it will,
but never persuade.

20. Rains and desire

All the memories rushed through her mind as she felt
those first drops of rain
it wasn't just about those moments
which she had lived
it was also about those moments
which she had always desired to live
yet again, she was mesmerized by the magic of rain
yet again, she wanted to be all by herself
to be embraced by the person
who was her first thought
when she woke up in the morning
being as peaceful as the rays of the sun
as reliving as an evening breeze
If only she could tell him
that for her he was
a dream, a puzzle, a bliss
her most favourite unfulfilled wish.

21. CLOSURE

It's the continuous juggle between our heart and mind
That keeps the hope of togetherness, between two lives
entwined
Though the tumultuous rush of thoughts instigates us to
move away,
our fragile fervent feelings always finds a reason to stay
This constant struggle that we encounter with ourselves
Makes us doubt, even the worth of one-self
The fondness which was supposed to make us feel
heavenly
We start avoiding it and no longer want to crave for it
intensely
Until the confusion struck us, for the umpteen times,
again
Tempting us to give it yet another chance,
from which we tried, but could never refrain
But the truth is, somewhere down the line, we all know
our answers
Still, secretly hoping it to be untrue, as if living a known
lie,

because all of us just desire to be loved
and in today's time, that's how we self pamper
Our expectations never fail to fade, we don't even want
them to persuade
Our souls keep crying aloud,
and that's what we ourselves have endowed
We even agree to settle for less,
although knowing that we deserve the best
We tend to find our happiness in the deserted islands,
even if, it's an iota of what we want
Leaving behind those dense forests,
which are willing to shower tonnes of it,
even when it is without our want.
Howsoever bitter the reality is,
it will keep haunting you,
Until you accept it
and it knocks you down completely
But, after the final downfall,
when we rise, we will see ourselves altogether
differently.
It will be an experience of earned and yearned
composure
And that, everyone, will be our ultimate CLOSURE.

9 789370 923515